The Twelfth Book of Mischief

Poems by

Pamela Martin

The Twelfth Book of Mischief
Copyright 2008 by Pamela Gowan

All rights reserved under International and Pan-American copyright conventions. No part of this book may be reproduced, stored in a retrieval system or transmitted in any form, electronic, mechanical, or by any other means, without written permission of the author.

Illustrated by Kathleen Hardy.

International Standard Book Number: 978-0-615-26193-5

Table of Contents

Part I

The Twelfth Book of Mischief 9
Nemesis 9
Love and Fear 9
The Enabler 10
Us 10
Chattel 10
The Masseuse 11
Merciful 12
Litigation 12
Waterboarding 12
Court-ship 13
Juicy Juice 14
P.A,M. 14
Underachiever 14
Exhumation! 15
Bedtime Prayer 16
Chef d'oeuvre 16
"Petoria" 16
Cheshire Pam 17
Prescription for Greatness 18
Swinging Both Ways 18
"Senator for Life" 18
Onomatopoeia: Silence 19
The Acting Precedent 20
A Living Will 20
Recidivism 20
The *Yenta* 21
Misogyny 21
Pussy Whipped 21
Glossolalia 22
The Cat's "Meow" 22
Canine-ization 23
A.D.D. 23
A Complimentary Color 23
Generous to a Fault 24
Compassionate to a Fault 24
A Growing Problem 24

Part II

The Wrath of Agamemnon	27
Faith without Work is Dead	27
A Rosy Outlook	27
Naughty *and* Nice	28
An Erstwhile Friend	28
Summer, Highland Falls (2008)	28
The Ascension	29
Intemperance	30
Pray, Tell	30
Eternal Life?	30
The Elixir of Life	31
Rambling Rose	32
The Noble Prize	32
Linguistics	32
Strings Attached	33
Revisionism: Failure to Launch (first reading)	34
Revisionism: Failure to Launch (second reading)	34
Revisionism: Failure to Launch (third reading)	34
"Smile for the Camera"	35
Fame: The Eschewal	36
Fame: Passion	36
Fame: Ambivalence	36
An Epicurean Reflection	37
The Clandestine Life	38
Clairvoyance	38
John 3:16	38
Horizontal Dancing	39
Dyspepsia	39
When Good Cats Do Nothing	39
Acrophobia	40
Neo-Platonism	40
"The Ghost of Christmas Past"	40
The Daley[2] Paean	41
My Manual of Style	41
Freudian	41

Part III

Revelations 45
The Capitulation 45
L—o—n—g—i—n—g 45
Who knew? 46
The Wasteland 46
Prophylaxis 46
Telekinesis 47
Internecine Warfare 48
Insomnia Cures Insomnia 48
Watchwords 48
Sirius 49
Deciduous Trees 50
Rite of Passage 50
Windows to the Soul 50
Leverage 51
Billy the Kid 52
"Speed Demon" 52
Intelligent Life 52
Sansculottes 53
"Comfort" Food 54
D.U.I. 54
Call of the Wild 54
Phaeton 55
The Vortex of History 56
Pulchritude 56
The Insouciant Gaul 56
Too Great Thinkers 57
Do Cats Go to Heaven? 57
"The *Belle* of Amherst" 57
Living in the Past 58
Sisters 58
Affairs of the Heart 58
Lucky 59
Lacerations 59
A Sex Symbol 59

Part I

The Twelfth Book of Mischief

I have a duo-decagon
And a duodenum.
But they can't save me from myself
Living in this slum.
I will take a dozen eggs
And put them in a sock.
Then I will meet you at high noon
Or at twelve o'clock.

Nemesis

I took a trip on LSD.*
I remember when
I was young and had no sense
With no "compunctioning."
Now I am old and cannot see
What I did see then.
All I know is at the time
You were still my friend.

*i.e. Lake Shore Drive.

Love and Fear

The fear of God has given man
His caution and concern
For what is good and what is right
Because He is so stern.
The love of God has saved mankind
From a death it knows is certain.
But for him we all would die
At the final curtain.

The Enabler

I took you for granted.
That was my mistake.
And I do accept
It was mine to make.
I hasten to add
You are at fault, too.
I could not have done it
Without help from you.

Us

Feral means "wild."
Domestic means "tame."
Shakespeare once asked,
"What's in a name?"
Naming is something
We have to do
To distinguish between
A "me" and a "you."

Chattel

A pain in the neck.
A pain in the ass.
A pain in a place
You don't want to ask.
A pain is the one thing
You don't want to have.
It treats you like you are
Its personal slave.

The Masseuse

My hands never tire
Of massaging your fur.
No one I know
Would ever incur
The time and the money
I put into you.
But there is nothing else
I'd rather do.

Merciful

It is what it is.
It's not what it's not.
We are who we are
Or have you forgot
What it means to be human,
What it means to live,
What it means to be Christian,
What it means to forgive?

Litigation

I will take you to task.
I will take you to court
The result of which
I have to report
It will leave you penuirious,
It will leave you distressed
And, in the end,
It will make you depressed.

Waterboarding

Sweeter than nothing.
Sweeter than corn.
Why is it always
I'm so forlorn?
Maybe it's something
I won't confess
Unless I am put
Under duress.

Court-ship

It sure took a long time
For me to say "I do"
And, when I did,
I was such a fool.
But I must say
I learned my lesson well.
Now I can say,
"You can go to hell."

Juicy Juice

Food is like sex,
A carnal desire.
I must admit
It sets me on fire.
But whenever I
Eat from the apple,
I must admit
I prefer Snapple.

P.A.M.*

Just yesterday
I googled my name.
Now there is something
I have to explain.
Pamela Martin
Is a great poet.
It's just that for now
Nobody knows it.

*Pamela Ann Martin. Throughout its history, "Pamela" was a popular name in the South. Among my many namesakes was Ann Pamela Cunningham, (my mother was dyslexic) the founder of the Mount Vernon Ladies Association, who saved George Washington's sacred home from certain destruction during the Civil War. But for her there would be no Mount Vernon today.

Underachiever

They showed me the mountains.
They showed me the sea.
They gave me high honors
At the U. of C.
But as a student
I was quite poor.
My reading assignments
I would ignore.

Exhumation!

A man is a man
Unless he's alone.
Then he is something
More like a drone.
A woman is a woman
Until she is married.
Then you would say
She has been buried.

Bedtime Prayer

Pill, oh! Pill, oh!
Help me to sleep.
Help me relax
And finally retreat
From the worries and cares
That I encumber.
Allay my fears
And put them asunder.

*Chef d'oeuvre**

Sometimes I feel
Like a vending machine
That is used constantly
And never kept clean.
A chef or a sous
I may not be
But, in the end,
They are healthy.

*Fr., a masterpiece.

"Petoria"

"Vitiate the proletariat!"
I love the *Family Guy*.
So much so, I have to say
That is no lie.
I watch him every evening
After the world news
Which helps explain the refrain:
"I will not recuse!"

Cheshire Pam

My smile is congenital.
I got it at birth
Which helps to explain
My myriad mirth.
But it doesn't explain
Why I have no hearth
And suffer at times
From lower self-worth.

Prescription for Greatness

I am no chameleon.
I will stand my ground
At any provocation
Like a junkyard hound.
A vigilante I am not.
I even loathe the thought.
I do my best in every way.
I do that which I ought.

Swinging Both Ways

In New England there are many churches
But Robert Frost loved his birches.
I do not know why.
If it weren't for central heating,
Air conditioning and padded seating
I, too, would touch the sky.

"Senator for Life"

The cat's got my tongue
But I got its tail.
The tail wags the dog.
The dog goes to jail.
The bird gets the worm.
The worm is hermaphroditic.
He lost the race
At Chappaquiddick.

Onomatopoeia: Silence*

*It goes without saying.

The Acting Precedent

In the end I may pretend
To be what I am not.
But, in review, that's nothing new
Or have you forgot?
History "repeats" itself,
Said the noble sage.
We are all but actors.
All the world's a stage.

A Living Will

"Suicide is painless"
If what they say is true.
I have never tried it
But I think I do
Keep it as an option
As a last resort.
Remember this gravely
When I'm on life-support.

Recidivism

I'm looking for Jack!
Where did he go?
Probably somewhere
I would not know.
If it wasn't for Jack,
Jack, the jackhammer,
I'd probably be
Back in the slammer.

The *Yenta**

People will tell you
It is all right
To pick up a stranger
And spend the night.
But what people tell you
May not be right,
So I go to synagogue
Every Saturday night.

*Yiddish, literally, "one that meddles;" a matchmaker.

Misogyny

We took to the streets
In support of our cause
For which we earned
No dearth of applause.
If we were wrong
(They think we were),
Do like the others.
Blame it on "her."

Pussy Whipped

Johnny Carson
Was a funny man.
Surely I was
His biggest fan.
He proved to the world
That he was no wussy
When he asked Raquel*
If he could pet her pussy (cat).

*Raquel Welch, famous mid-twentieth century "icon."

Glossolalia*

Every day is "Pet Your Pet Day"
At the Martin House.
Martin Luther did proclaim it
As did Ricard Strauss.
St. Francis of Assisi+
Preached to all the birds.
If I contradict him,
They'd be my final words.

*Gk., speaking in tongues.

+Founder of the Franciscan Order of the Catholic Church. He was born in Italy in 1181/2 and died in 1226. His father was Professor of Sartorial Sciences at Ornithology University (Assisi). He earned a Master's of Social Work at the University of Bologna in 1205. At a very early age, he obsessed about the fact that birds had no clothes. After his valiant but unsuccessful attempts to get them to "suit up," he opened the Wildlife Sanctuary for Nudists which has been in continuous operation since then and is now part of the World Nudist Coalition headquartered at the University of Chicago's International Politics Interdisciplinary Committee, which was founded by Saul Bellow and Milton Friedman in 1976 (the year they won their Nobel prizes for literature and economics respectively) on the South side of Chicago. A M.S.W. is a terrible thing to waste.

The Cat's "Meow"

My cats are quite amusing.
They speak in a high-pitched voice.
To them I am their mother.
I am their only choice.
I serenade them in falsetto.
They think I'm a cat.
That's how you treat your children
If you want to chat.

Canine-ization

A friend is someone you can trust
And will hold your hand.
He'll stay with you through thick and thin
And make you understand
That enemies may come and go
But you will stand by him
And will never leave
At the slightest whim.

A.D.D.*

I am a lexicographer
Who writes trite poetry.
I do it for attention.
Sometimes I can't see
There is method to my madness,
A methodology.
I want all the world
To come and look at me.

*Eng., acronym for "attention deficit disorder."

A Complimentary Color

Fishing for a compliment
Is as old as time.
They say self-deprecation
Is more potent than fine wine
If it can elicit
A kind word or two
That can make the difference
When you're feeling blue.

Generous to a Fault

What can make a Liberal
Give up the friendly ghost
Of those expectations
That he loves the most?
There really is no answer
If what they say is true.
A liberal is a liberal.
There's nothing you can do.

Compassionate to a Fault

What can make a Conservative
Give up the friendly ghost
Of those expectations
That he loves the most?
There really is no answer
If what they say is true.
A conservative is a conservative.
There's nothing you can do.

A Growing Problem

I'm prostrate on my prostate.
What's a man to do?
It just keeps getting bigger.
I haven't got a clue.
I'm going to the bathroom.
For the twenty-seventh time.
But my doctor reassures me
I am doing fine.

Part II

The Wrath of Agamemnon

I just lost my temper
But I know it's not lost.
It will be back tomorrow
But, God knows, at what cost.
To those who claim to know me
Know when I am mad
Nothing can control me.
I am the perfect cad.

Faith without Work is Dead

Our Faith was a thrifty girl
She saved all her money.
But now it seems that she's about
To run out of honey.
The winding unemployment line
Just keeps getting longer.
Now she takes a plane
To stave off her hunger.

A Rosy Outlook

She works so hard at camouflage
She rarely has the time
To care for matters close at heart.
It really is a crime.
Life's for those who take time
To smell all the roses.
That is why they keep them
Right under their noses.

Naughty *and* Nice

My poetry is part of me
And I'm a part of it.
I look around. What do I see?
I'm a real halfwit.
My better half, if he exists,
(as yet I am not "whole")
Will not care a single wit
If Santa brings me coal.

An Erstwhile Friend

Hindsight is 20/20.
Foresight is quite blind.
It's easier to see
What is left behind.
You have me in your vision.
You have me in your ken.
You're the only one
Who knew me way back when…

Summer, Highland Falls (2008)

"It's de ja vu all over again,"
I said to the man
Who was sitting next to me,
"Without the Can-Can."
I may never find my muse,
But this much I can say:
"Life's a Cabaret, old chum.
Come to the Cabaret."

The Ascension

I'm a victim of circumstance.
I don't have the will
To get up in the morning
And take in my fill
Of what life has to offer
Over that Great Hill.
I stumble down the other side
Just like Jack and Jill.

Intemperance

You may want to change me
But you can't change yourself.
It doesn't matter anyway.
I'll drink to your health.
I am sorry if you think
I have been unkind.
Drinking is the only way
I can totally unwind.

Pray, Tell

What difference does it make
If you win or lose?
It's all the same in the end.
Which one would you choose?
Questions without answers
Are questions nonetheless.
If you don't know the answer,
Would you, please, confess?

Eternal Life?

A cat has nine lives.
We have but one.
When it is all over
It's as good as done.
A second life may be had
For those who do believe
In miracles and such things
But they may be deceived.

The Elixir of Life

They say the toughest battle
Is the one you wage within
That makes you so defensive
And punishes you for sin.
To me that is offensive.
But this much is true:
Nothing can defeat you
After you have had a few.

Rambling Rose

I know I may be a fool
But really does it matter?
It really is enough for me
To engage in endless chatter.
I'm a Lady Chatterly.
What is the real harm
If I drop by on the way
To the family farm?

The Noble Prize

When you look around you
What is it you see?
Abjection and rejection
Or sweet charity?
What you see is what you get.
Each of us is free.
And there is in each of us
A great nobility.

Linguistics

There's something in the meaning
Of each and every word
That gives it ambiguity
And makes it sound absurd.
Words are just like people.
They're fickle as can be.
They bend under pressure
And have no integrity.

Strings Attached

Would you believe when I was ten
(As much as I remember then)
I played second fiddle
As I danced around the griddle.
Now I play the first violin
In Orchestra Hall for Gwendolyn.
Out of the frying pan into the fire.
But, frankly, I prefer the lyre.

Revisionism

Failure to Launch (First Reading)

If anything is sacred
It would be your health.
This comes from someone who has lost it
If I say so myself.
There's a wealth of information
To buttress my case.
I'm a living product
Of the cult of teenage waste.

Failure to Launch (Second Reading)

If anything is sacred
It would be your health.
This comes from someone who has lost it
If I say so myself.
There's a wealth of information
To buttress my case.
I'm a living product
Of the cult of teenage waste.

Failure to Launch (Third Reading)

If anything is sacred
It would be your health.
This comes from someone who has lost it
If I say so myself.
There's a wealth of information
To buttress my case.
I'm a living product
Of the cult of teenage waste.

Ad infinitum*

*Latin, "to infinity."

"Smile for the Camera"

I told you once (and I repeat)
I'll not tell you again.
I've come too far to be a star
To settle or pretend
That what I want can be found
In this homely town.
To make it big wear a wig
And put away that frown.

Fame

The Eschewal*

Public life is something
I can live without.
Privacy is something
That is paramount.
People who want glory
Will never understand.
Politics was never
Part of my life plan.

*cf. When Good Cats Do Nothing, (p. 39).

Passion

The plans we make
Are seldom spoken.
The loves we share
Are often broken.
But what lives on
Is the desire
To meet the one
You set on fire.

Ambivalence

I never wanted to be a poet
(and you can see why).
But that never stopped me.
Either do or die.
If I have been successful,
The success was bittersweet.
I only tried my best
Never to repeat.

An Epicurean Reflection

Mirror, mirror on the tape deck,
What is it you see?
When I look around the room
I think you see me.
Do I look like Medusa
With a stone cold heart?
Or like someone you remember
Who's in love with art?

The Clandestine Life

Words are only ciphers
Deciphering the code
Of human conduct
And lightening the load
Of the isolation
We feel deep inside
That can overcome us
As we run and hide.

Clairvoyance

Some people see tomorrow
As clear as Claritin.
But all I see is sorrow
And guilt for all my sins.
I was touched by an angel
Who looked at me and said:
"All's the world's a stage.
Tread lightly where you tread."

John 3:16*

They sent me to Obedience Training.
They called it Sunday school.
They drilled into to my impressionable head
To live the Golden Rule.
I cherish this education.
It is all I got.
God knows it is the only thing
I have not forgot.

*The Bible (KJV), "For God so loved the world that he gave his only begotten son for whosoever believieth in Him shall not perish but have everlasting life."

Horizontal Dancing

Without a trace.
Without a scar.
If I look up,
I'll go far.
But the only place
I'd rather be
Is lying with you
Next to me.

Dyspepsia

To love or be loved?
That is the question
That burns in my soul
And helps my digestion.
Can you have it both ways?
That's a suggestion
I would pursue
To cure indigestion.

When Good Cats Do Nothing*

Life has been good to me.
I can walk and I can see.
But it is sheer hypocrisy
To see evil and let it be.*

*cf. Fame: The Eschewal, (p. 36).

Acrophobia

I'm not afraid of many things
But I'm afraid to die.
Life has been so good to me
I do not know why
It has to end so senselessly
Or even end at all.
I rue day of Adam's apple
And life after the Fall.

Neo-Platonism

When a school of thought suggests to me
That I can meet my maker.
"How is it so?" I ask myself,
"I'm no 'mover and a shaker.'"
The ephemeral and eternal
Coalesce on my mainframe.
The-more-things-change
The more they stay the same.

"The Ghost of Christmas Past"

September babies are Christmas presents.
Just count back nine months.
I'm September 20th.
I am not a dunce.
Mom and dad were active
Under the mistletoe.
I should know 'cuz I was there
Twenty years ago.

The Daley² Paean

A fertile imagination
Begets, begets, begets.
We begat this paean
So nobody forgets
We have made Chicago
What it is today
We have made Chicago
Out of sand and clay.

My Manual of Style

I know every cliché in the book.
I have coined a few.
If you put your mind to it,
I know you can, too.
As a numismatist,
I am proud to say
I use worn out clichés
Each and every day.

Freudian

You're sitting on this suitcase
Waiting for the day
When he comes to marry you
And take you away.
But the baggage that you carry
Is with you all the time.
You *can* take it with you
Especially at bedtime.

Part III

Revelations

Something was revealed today
That was once unknown.
I put it in a teleplay.
How quickly it has grown.
You might be too skeptical
To admit forsooth
I'm more popular than the queen.
That's the Gospel truth.

The Capitulation

I provide the levity.
But all you want is brevity.
So for my longevity
I cease and desist.
But no matter how you cry
(I don't know the reason why)
I bow to the *vox populi**
And do not persist.

*Latin, "voice of the people."

L—o—n—g—i—n—g

Now it's time for me to say
It's time to go our separate ways.
May that way be long or short
You must give a full report
Of what happened on that day
You took my heart away....

Who Knew?

I knew
You knew
They knew
We knew.

The Wasteland

The words danced upon the page
Like raindrops on a pane
Falling, oh, so gently
Like the rain in Spain.
When I look around me
(Much to my disdain)
I can't help but wonder
Where is this fruited plain?

Prophylaxis

My shoes serve to cover
My sensitive feet.
I walk upon them
When I cross the street.
They're made of fine leather
So soft and so warm.
I need them always
To keep me from harm.

Telekinesis

I can move this heavy chair.
All I have to do is stare.
I can place it over there
Without a shirtsleeve.
If mind-over-matter was a hoax
I, my friend, would have to coax
You as hard as common folks
For you disbelieve.

Internecine Warfare

I reached out to touch
Those unseemly bounds
That separate us from
The dogs and the hounds.
What I soon discovered
Surprised even me.
The hounds acted like the soldiers
I saw on TV.

Insomnia Cures Insomnia

I didn't sleep at all last night.
But I surely will tonight.
That will curb my appetite
And close my eyes without a fight.

Watchwords

Men fear women
Who are strong.
Women fear men
Who are wrong.

Always fear fear.
Always hate hate.
Always take time
To celebrate!

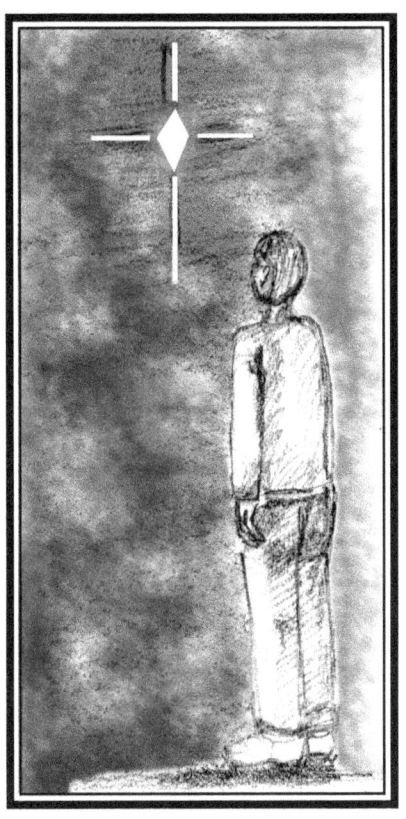

Sirius*

A man without a past
Is a man without romance.
A man without a future
Will not get a second chance.
But a man who has the presence
To do that which is right
Will be rewarded in the heavens
With a star upon the night.

*a.k.a. the *Dog Star*, the brightest star in the night-time sky. Serious.

Deciduous Trees

The rustling and the murmur
Of the doomed leaves
(It goes without saying)
Can bring me to my knees.
But the raking and the burning
Leaves an aftertaste
As unpleasant as the making
Of a landfill waste.

Rite of Passage

We may not pass this way again.
Remember how it looks
Because it is the sort of thing
You won't find in books.
Always take the scenic route
Wherever you may go.
Kodachrome is your best friend,
Time's your greatest foe.

Windows to the Soul

Her eyes are green. Her eyes are brown.
They can see without a sound.
They grow with maturity
And give them personality.

Leverage

When I pulled the lever down
It hit me in the eye.
I have to say it hurt so much
I began to cry.
When you pull the lever down
Here's what you should do:
Run real fast. Don't slow down.
Don't-let-it-catch-you!

Billy the Kid*

You have been a "(e)scapegoat"
For a worthy cause.
You have a place in heaven,
An ovation and applause.
You have been an outlaw.
(There was a lot at stake.)
Surrender at the courthouse
Before your life they take.

*a.k.a. William Atrim or William H. Bonney (d. 1881), a notorious ruffian in the American West. He killed many men and loved many women.

"Speed Demon"

I'm hitting all my cylinders
(I have a V-8).
I'm flying down the corridor
Hurling like a freight.
Slow doesn't seem to be
Something I can do.
I must say that, if I could,
I would not want to.

Intelligent Life

An interplanetary probe
Is seeking alien life
Because they think it must exist
Along with war and strife.
We know, in fact, it does exist.
We hear it on the news
Unless we have been duped again
By this simple ruse.

*Sansculottes**

Did you see the Patriot act?
He sure as hell can't dance
Around the living room with grace
In those baggy pants.
If I were to say to you
Culottes were the style
In a simpler place and time,
You would only smile.

*Fr., "without knee-breeches (lower class apparel)."

"Comfort" Food

Lead on, Sammy! Lead on, Tabby!
To your water bowl.
I think it's good advice
To have a simple goal.
You may find that when you dine
The cubbard is now bare.
You're not alone. Just telephone.
You'll find some comfort there.

D.U.I.

Over the limit. Under arrest.
If you are ever
Put to the test
And fail to establish
Your sobriety.
Don't think, "It never
Could happen to me."

Call of the Wild

Click it or ticket it.
Stick it or prick it.
Flick the black cricket
Onto the floor.
If you can tip it
But cannot flip it,
You will most surely
Hear the bug roar.

Phaeton*

I am photophobic.
I can't stand the light.
In the brightest hour
I want only night.
It's as if poor Helios,
(Greek god of the sun),
Lost his sense of humor
And his only son.*

*Phaeton, Helios' son, lost control of his father's "fiery chariot in the sky," and was struck dead by a thunderbolt thrown by Zeus, the supreme god in Greek mythology.

The Vortex of History

They say it's a circle.
(Some say it's not)
Or a straight line
Made up of dots.
I say it's a gyre
Spinning around
As it gently
Slides on the ground.

Pulchritude

Beauty is skin deep
(I know it's true)
The color of your skin dictates
What you can and cannot do.
Sleeping Beauty (in a trance)
Excited all the fellas
With her necrophilia.
She was a *Rosa Bella*.

The Insouciant Gaul

The Frenchman labels everything
With a carefree guile.
You can't say it. You can't spell it.
Go that extra mile.
I admire from afar
Their perfume and their food.
They perfected everything
Especially the nude.

Too Great Thinkers

Horace Greeley was the father
Of a liberal school.
In the West he encouraged
The growth of sovereign rule.
"Wander" Greeley never had a thought
He did not publish.
I should know for I must go
And read all of his rubbish.

Do Cats Go to Heaven?

That is the age old question
For which there is no clue.
They're on there way to heaven.
(I have known a few.)
Although they do no know it
And are unaware,
They're already in heaven.
They haven't got a care.

"The *Belle** of Amherst"

Death to her+ was gripping.
It almost was alive.
It was her one obsession
It helped her to survive.
She had short but sweet encounters
With other subjects, too.
God knows, in her place and time
There was nothing else to do.

*Fr., the "beauty" of Amherst.
+Emily Dickinson (1830 -1886), nineteenth century American poet.

Living in the Past

Time passes, oh, so slowly
When you're thinking of
How quickly it will pass
When you are in love.
But they did not tell you
That it will not last
And that you'll spend most of your time
Living in the past.

Sisters

I can mimic anyone.
God has not forgot
To turn the record off.
But Emily I'm not.
When history repeats itself
(As stuck in a groove),
Repetition is the mother of learning
A century removed.

Affairs of the Heart

Some may call it unwise
But I am not ashamed
To admit to anyone
I was not to blame
For the outcome and the curse
Of our love affair.
I only wish
I did not care.

Lucky

A lucky streak.
A lucky strike.
A lucky trend
Is my delight.
As luck would have it
(Even so)
My luck ran out.
Don't you know.

Lacerations

Sheltered and defensive
I lead a troubled life.
Esconced in self-protection
I dare not suffer strife.
You may not believe it.
I am not a wife.
When love is torn asunder
It cuts like a knife.

A Sex Symbol

Tactless and oppressive,
Priapus* was his name.
This we know for certain
He's the one to blame
For our promiscuous behavior
And our fertility
And do not forget
Our cupidity.

*The ugly Roman god with huge genitals who promoted fertility.

Publications by *Pamela Martin*

Pamela Martin published thirteen books of light verse between the years 2004 and 2008 as follows:

The Twelfth Book of Mischief/A Baker's Dozen, Inkwell Press, Chicago, Illinois, (2008). B/w illustrated by Kathleen Hardy.

Parameters, Inkwell Press, Chicago, Illinois, (2008). Color illustrated by Kathleen Hardy.

American Realism, Inkwell Press, Chicago, Illinois, (2008). B/w illustrated by Kathleen Hardy.

Myopia, Inkwell Press, Chicago, Illinois, (2008). B/w illustrated by Kathleen Hardy.

Levitations, Inkwell Press, Chicago, Illinois, (2007). B/w illustrated by Kathleen Hardy.

The Beauty of It All, Inkwell Press, Chicago, Illinois, (2007).

One Hundred Poems, Adams Press, Chicago, Illinois, (2006).

A Moral Dilemma, Watermark Press, Owings Mills, Maryland, (2006).

Clueless, Watermark Press, Owings Mills, Maryland, (2005).

Carpe Diem, Watermark Press, Owings Mills, Maryland, (2005).

Live! Watermark Press, Owings Mills, Maryland, (2005).

Promises to Keep, Watermark Press, Owings Mills, Maryland, (2004).

The End

Publications by *Pamela Martin*

Pamela Martin published thirteen books of light verse between the years 2004 and 2008 as follows:

The Twelfth Book of Mischief/A Baker's Dozen, Inkwell Press, Chicago, Illinois, (2008). B/w illustrated by Kathleen Hardy.

Parameters, Inkwell Press, Chicago, Illinois, (2008). Color illustrated by Kathleen Hardy.

American Realism, Inkwell Press, Chicago, Illinois, (2008). B/w illustrated by Kathleen Hardy.

Myopia, Inkwell Press, Chicago, Illinois, (2008). B/w illustrated by Kathleen Hardy.

Levitations, Inkwell Press, Chicago, Illinois, (2007). B/w illustrated by Kathleen Hardy.

The Beauty of It All, Inkwell Press, Chicago, Illinois, (2007).

One Hundred Poems, Adams Press, Chicago, Illinois, (2006).

A Moral Dilemma, Watermark Press, Owings Mills, Maryland, (2006).

Clueless, Watermark Press, Owings Mills, Maryland, (2005).

Carpe Diem, Watermark Press, Owings Mills, Maryland, (2005).

Live! Watermark Press, Owings Mills, Maryland, (2005).

Promises to Keep, Watermark Press, Owings Mills, Maryland, (2004).

The End

The Rust Belt

Vivid are the memories
Of me and you.
But gone are all the reveries
That I once knew.
Daydreams turn into nightmares.
Love turns into lust.
I can't do anything.
In God I rust.

Xenophobia

A stranger is merely someone
Who you do not know.
And he is that someone
You only wish would go.
You do not want to know him
As you know yourself.
We are all but strangers
Drinking to our health.

That's That

"May you live in interesting times,"
The Chinese proverb states.
How can we not feign
An interest in our fates?
Life is far too curious
Even for a cat.
This I know for certain.
And that, my friend, is that.

Obsequiousness

I have only this small gift
To set before the Lord.
Bestowed on me at birth
(With my umbilical cord),
The talent that I have
Won't impress the many
But I am satisfied
If He enjoys it any.

Stop the Bull!

It's a forgone conclusion
Time passes by too quickly.
And the rose on the bush
Can be rather prickly.
What I mean to say
Is to take life by the horns.
And always endeavor
Not to be forlorn.

Love: The Overture

I did not recognize you
When I met you on the street
On that cold, dark evening
When we chanced to meet.
"Should old acquaintance be forgot."
I hope I'm not one.
But what you once meant to me
Is now long gone.

"A Draw"

For every opportunity
There is a dead end.
And clearly "affirmation"
May not be your closest friend.
It takes away your dignity
And your knowledge of self-worth
But corrects the disadvantages
You inherited at birth.

Deaf Ears

I laid down the gauntlet
When you said goodbye.
What's the use in fighting
When you want to cry?
Although they try to cheer me up,
I simply turn away
And do not listen to
A single word they say.

Unfathomable

I ruminate and cogitate
That it is right
To squander our existence
And advance the plight
Of the evil and the wicked
Who enjoy the oversight
Of the weak and of the weary
Who are too innumerable to cite.

"I Know"

I know what to say, and I say it.
I know what to do, and I do it.
I know what to think, and I think it.
I know what to believe, and I believe it.

Salvation

We are on probation for a crime
We do regret.
St. Peter wrote the penal code
So we would not forget
To ask for spiritual healing
And to finally intercede.
It's just like Him to save us
In our hour of need.

The Wisdom of the Ages

History is liberation
From the tenets of the past.
Each day is a new day
When you're free at last.
But if it is nonbinding,
What is it good for?
It goes without saying
There is no forevermore.

Static Cling

My Philosophy (1988)

The road is long and winding.
It was a long time ago.
Nothing here is binding.
Go with the flow.
Swimming upstream, I have learned,
Is a very foolish thing.
And no one knows for certain
What tomorrow will bring.

My Philosophy (1998)

The road is long and winding.
It was a long time ago.
Nothing here is binding.
Go with the flow.
Swimming upstream, I have learned,
Is a very foolish thing.
And no one knows for certain
What tomorrow will bring.

My Philosophy (2008)

The road is long and winding.
It was a long time ago.
Nothing here is binding.
Go with the flow.
Swimming upstream, I have learned,
Is a very foolish thing.
And no one knows for certain
What tomorrow will bring.

A Baker's Dozen

"Muy caliente! Muy caliente!"
Is what the baker said.
I know this much for certain
He makes a damn, fine bread.
In his measuring system
A "dozen" is thirteen.
Even a trixadecaphobe
Knows that's what he means.

Historiography* as "Ancestuousness"+

You have slept in silence
For one hundred years.
Although you did not know it,
I shed many tears
For a generation
That was once alive.
Its values and ideals
Could not long survive.

*The "history of history." +Noun, neologism for "ancestor worship" derived from the noun "ancestor" and the adjective "incestuous."

The Starter Wife

Do you love me for my money?
Do you love me for my fame?
Do you really love me?
If so, please, explain
Why you told your mother
That I was a skank.
If you amount to anything,
You have me to thank.

The Lonely Night

I can't believe it's over.
It has been four years
Since I started writing.
Despite my darkest fears.
It could have been much better.
But it turned out all right.
Yet, at times, I think that life
Is one long, lonely night.

Shortchanged

We each live on an island
Separated at birth.
Yet we are loosely tethered
Enjoying the warm hearth.
If there was a reason
We were put on earth,
I do not believe
He got his money's worth.

"A Lucky Seven"*

Young Republicans want their money.
Old Republicans want true love.
I myself prefer
None of the above.
Once the "Party of Lincoln,"
Reagan stole their hearts.
But John McCain can personally boost
Those sagging housing starts.

*During the presidential campaign of 2008, it came to light that the Republican candidate, John McCain, owned seven "houses" (i.e. houses and condominiums) around the country. At the time he was first asked, he didn't know how many he actually owned! It is said McCain's second wife, Cindy, inherited $100 million.

In God's Image?

The Fauves* are out to get me,
Those terrible, wild beasts.
They only want to roast me
And serve me as a feast.
I don't listen to
A single word they say.
Now I know for certain
Man was made from clay.

*Fr., the "wild beasts;" a modern art movement at the turn of the twentieth century founded by the French artists Henri Mattisse (1869-1954) and Andre Derain (1880-1954).

"Indefatigable"

It only takes ten minutes
To play "string" with Tab.
She loves the thrill of winning
And it makes her sad
To see it end so quickly.
(She has done her best.)
But she puts away her toy
And gives me a rest.

Global Warming ☺

I'm so old I can remember
How cold it was in December.
That's why I had a special coat.
It was so big it made me float.
But I liked it just the same.
So much so I can't complain.
I no longer need it not.
It is so warm. I like it hot.

Etudes

1: Metaphor and Simile as Autobiography

I'm as blind as bat.
Sly as fox.
Free as a bird.
Stubborn as an ox.

2: The End of Slavery

The Egyptians invented cotton.
Tonic is mixed with gin.
Eli put them together
To make the "cotton gin."

3: Only On a First-Name Basis

I am glad to know you.
I only know your name.
But if we get any closer
I will go insane.

4: An Isolated Incident

It happened only once.
It won't happen again.
It will not be repeated.
It was my only sin.

5: "2x Shy": The Birth of Cynicism

I was totally committed
To a worthy cause
But it bit me in the ass,
This with no applause.

"The Do-Gooder"

I am full of kindness
And Christian charity.
I touch the lives of those I love
With magnanimity.
But as I look into the mirror
When the day is done,
I tell myself "I am so good.
It was so much fun."

Recognizance

I am living proof
I am quite alive.
And I am proof perfect
That is not a lie.
I stand here before you
With my hat in hand
Trying to convince you
I should not get remand.

Trust Issues

I rue the day I met you.
I woe the day you died.
But it did not upset me
Although indeed I cried.
More love is lost through folly.
More love is lost through lust.
But more love is lost though loving
Someone you can't trust.

Fat Cats, Jr.*

Sam wants what she can't have.
Tab has what she don't want.
They haves and the have-nots
Call them termagants.
If I took away
Their Crunchies and their Pounce,
They would waste away
Slowly by the ounce.

*cf. Fat Cats, Sr, (p. 13).

The Piano Man

I sometimes push the envelope
A little bit too far.
But I don't care. As they say,
Someday I'll go far.
But, as it is, it's just me
At this old piano
Playing tunes and sipping wine
Wearing a sombrero.

Callousness

Rich folk, poor folk.
They're all the same to me.
We are all just people
With a history
Of random acts of kindness
Wrought from dark despair.
But I must admit
Sometimes we do not care.

The Visionary

I fomented a riot
Just by what I said.
I must best be careful
Or soon I will be dead.
They always shoot the messenger.
But I am here to stay.
You better listen to me
For I show the way.

Damaged Goods

It has come to my attention
You have gone away.
I know in my heart
You are gone to stay.
Despite our valiant efforts
To jettison the baggage
The best laid plans of mice and men
Are ruined by the damage.

A Cat's Heart

What I like most about my cats
Is that they're very dumb.
They speak not a single word
And do not suck their thumb.
But I know they love me
(And I love them so)
Because I feed them every day.
Just look. It does show.

The First Person Singular

How would you feel
When somebody says,
"You're not married.
You must be a 'les.'"
What if I am?
What if I'm not?
Those conversations
Are best soon forgot.

"Separate but Equal"

I prefer to live alone.
There's really not much to it.
Why that is is your best guess.
I cannot intuit.
People only bring you down.
I'm already there.
In the end, I say to you
Does anybody care?

Part III

A Profile in Courage

I worship at the feet
Of Robert Edward Lee,
Intrepid and undaunted,
With no temerity.
Robert fought the good fight.
But if he did not lose,
We would not be free today
Although we paid the dues.

Corpulence

Organic is the kind of food
I can live without.
I like food that makes you
Unhealthy and plain stout.
Obesity in humans
Is indeed loathsome
But, if it means more junk food,
I will fain succumb.

Polyglot

Northern Aggression or Southern Succession?
Call it what you will.
Either way you say it,
It was a bitter pill.
But we still fight this fight
To the present day.
Urban and rural.
It will not go away.

The Labyrinth of Life

I've failed at everything I've tried.
And I've tried everything.
I have disappointed some.
They are suffering.
But I know I have done my best
In each and every way.
It's just I am a ne'er-do-well
Who has lost her way.

A Better Life

To die of natural causes
Is to die a noble death.
Foul play is usually something
That makes your final breath
Seem sudden and unexpected,
Hasty and abrupt.
It goes without saying
This world is so corrupt.

"Dear"

You know I really loved you.
You could do no wrong.
No matter what you said or did
I would tag along.
But out of mind
We quickly became.
How could it be
I forgot your name?

Plate Tectonics

The Geological Survey
Knows a thing or two
About this ever-changing world
That's shifting under you.
Continental drifts
Are causing us great grief
Making mountains out of mole hills
And creating barrier reefs.

Recriminations

It is with great sorrow
That I say to you
Exactly what you said to me
Although it is not true
That I do not love you
Because you know I do.
No sooner than a word is spoken
It becomes untrue.

Died-in-the-Wool

I like burning bridges.
It is what I do
To end a situation
That I'm going through.
What lies in the future
Is rooted in the past.
And I hate to tell you
The dye has long been cast.

A Life Decision

I'm sorry for your loss.
I had a loss once, too.
It really does get better
In a day or two.
For now you will feel lonely
Without her by your side.
But you will soon feel better
If only you decide.

The Gaming Commission

You can't have it both ways
Unless they are the same.
If you did not know better,
You'd think I was insane.
But, when you think about it,
Tell me who's to blame
If you win or lose
When we play the game?

"The Impossible Dream"

Cigito ergo sum.*
I am, therefore I think
That it is unwise
To have another drink.
Just one is one too many.
Too many is just a few
Sobriety is something.
You should always do.

*Latin, "I think, therefore I am;" famous dictum of the French philosopher and mathematician, Rene Descartes (1596-1650).

Turning Back Time

When the day is done
I look at the clock
And wonder to myself
What have I forgot?
I know it's too late
To make up for lost time.
You never get it back.
It really is a crime.

A Fascist Ballad

I went to California
With a banjo on my knee.
I practiced every evening
Underneath a Redwood tree.
I sprinkled major sevenths
Throughout the melody
And sang a rousing chorus
Of "God save Queen Mary."

Infidel

Of all my hopes and selfish dreams
Only one came true.
I know inside my beating heart
That that one was you.
But you have been unfaithful
As the days go by.
I don't think you give a damn.
Why did you have to lie?

Am I Alive?

They say I was an accident
That fate would soon take back.
I did not mean to harm you
Or cause a heart attack.
I know you nearly killed me.
I'm hanging by a thread.
If life is what you make it,
I'm as good as dead.

Bunk Beds

I found an empty cardboard box
By the alley way.
I dragged it to the living room
For the cats to play.
Sammy looked in it.
Tabby made it home.
Sammy climbed on top
So Tab was not alone.

U. T. I.*

I'm so dumb
I cannot talk.
I'm so blind
I cannot see.
I'm so lame
I cannot walk.
I'm so pained
I cannot pee.

*Urinary Tract Infection

A Sympathy Vote

If I were you
And you were me,
You'd see what
I want to see.
I'd be what
You want to be.
We'd both learn
Real empathy.

Forewarned

You had me at hello.
You had me at goodbye.
You didn't have to go.
You didn't have to lie.
You didn't have to state
That you loved me so.
You didn't have to say
That you told me so.

The Love Train

I must say my train of thought
Is unhealthy.
I must confess in duress
It derails easily.
To stay on track and watch my back
I need from you
Unconditional love from up above
And that you stay true.

Limericks

The Hang Over

I'm ergophobic, indolent and lazy.
I must admit at times I go crazy.
But I'm crazy over you.
There is nothing I can do.
But right now, I admit, I'm a little hazy.

Homophobia

A homosexual is the kind of man
Who sticks his dingus in the can.
I do not approve
But I saw it in the Louvre.
It's something I do not understand.

Ich-Theology

I took a visit to the sea
When it suddenly came over me
The fish there all were dead.
They'd been shot inside the head,
A sad indictment of our great society.

"The Urge to Expand"

They say, "She* has an 'urge to the expand'
Onto her neighbor's homeland.'"
Although I do not know
If entirely it's so.
I look at Georgia+ and I see the quicksand.

*Russia. +The former Soviet republic of Georgia.

Queen Nefertiti*

The bust of Nefertiti
Lives in the Pergamon.
"Eich bin ein Berliner"
Who hails from Sagamon.
At first I did not notice.
(The guide drones on and on.)
One-eyed Nefertiti
Makes a good sermon.

*Nefertiti (1390 B.C.-1360 B.C.), queen of Egypt; putative (step)mother and mother-in-law of King Tutankhamun (King Tut).

Felicitations!

Plein air. Al fresco.
I love the outdoors!
Hunting and camping
And making hot s'mores.
But I can't deny
The electricity within.
When I met Felicity,
My life did begin.

Nocturnal Emission

Far from the ocean.
Near the Red Sea.
I can't believe
It happened to me.
I closed my eyes.
And what did I see?
A curvy lap dance
Sitting on me.

Funny Money (☺$$$)

Most of the time
The phone rings off the hook.
Most of the time
I think it's a crook
Trying to steal my money
To advance his pet cause.
I think it's funny
And give him applause.

"Pam's Best Friend"

Tabby reads the tabloids.
Sammy cannot read
For she is a dyslexic,
An extremely rare cat breed.
The world may never know
What I see in them.
But this much is for certain
They are my closest friends.

Dexter the Dexterous

I can take a blank page
And make it poetry.
You can take a canvas
And make the whole world see
That we are all but transients
Blinded by the night
Who can only try
To make a wrong a right.

Free Speech

I used to think of something
But it would take four days
For me to verbalize it
In a simple phrase.
But now I speak my mind
With spontaneity
Like my friend Rush Limbaugh
Extemporaneously.

The Reluctant Reformer

Moral support. Child Support.
It all the same to me.
But life support is what I need
To set my spirit free.
If you would, would you please
Kindly let me be?
In my heart I do my part
For society.

All Words

Al invented the internet.
I invented, "Don't ask. Don't tell."
Years before the military.
It wasn't a "hard sell"
To the shy and introverted
Child that I was
Who always knew the difference between
What she says and what she does.

"The Greatest Show on Earth"

You have great potential.
I know you'll go far.
But I can't say for certain
Exactly who you are.
Identity is something
That comes from within.
Someday you will thank me.
Let the show begin.

Audacity

I'm jealous of my prerogatives,
A real commitment-phobe.
I'm married to the notion
That we dare not probe
Into the human psyche
Lest we be apprised
That our darkest fears
Have been realized.

Part II

Abraham, Abraham

The only true government
Is the one that rules
The hearts of all its citizens
And uses it as tools
To make their lives incredible,
To be all they can be,
And forget their competition
And their rivalry.

Relapses

I remember yesterday
As if it were today.
I remember history
As if it were a day
In the life I once knew
That has gone away
And will never come again.
It is gone to stay.

I'll be damned!

Jaded and cynical,
I go through the day
Painfully conscious
That we cannot stay.
But I make the most of it
And I might as well
Because I know my bleeding heart
Is going straight to hell.

Anthropology 101

*Novis Homo**

Like the risen Phoenix,
I must truly say
I have risen from the ashes
To see another day.
Tomorrow may be better
(And it may be worse)
A pun is the lowest form of humor
But poetry is verse.

*Latin, literally the "new man," the American Adam—self-made and risen from the grave.

The American Adam

Adam and Eve did not leave
Until they were deported
From the Garden of Earthly Delights.
They had been supported
By the charity of the Church
With headquarters in Sweden.
By the way, I have to say
There is life after Eden.

The Greasy Spoon

Hopes and dreams and bubbling springs.
Tears on my eyelashes.
Tell the tale of diamond rings
Torn from satin sashes.
My only sin is I was born
With a sliver straw
Tucked inside my mouth.
It was my fatal flaw.

The Oedipus Complex

Who wants to solve the riddle,
The riddle of the Sphinx?
"I do," said poor Oedipus,
"I know what he thinks."
A man must kill his father
If he will be king
And satisfy his mother
With all worldly things.

"All the News that's Fit to Print"*

"Let the printers print!"
Is all I have to say.
Speaking your mind
Is the only way
To let somebody know
You were here today.
Freedom of the press
Is the only way.

*The motto of the *New York Times*.

Homer

I used to travel physically
To apprehend the time
When men walked about this earth
And filled their hearts with rhyme.
If I had been so fortunate
To be born so blind…
Now I sit here at my desk
And wonder what I'll find.

Twin Daughters of Different Litters

Sammy is so pretty.
But Tab's the intellect.
Isn't it a pity?
What would you expect?
We either live in comfort
Or abject poverty.
Either way the future
Is something we can't see.

The Family of Man

We are all distinguishable
By our DNA.
But we are all related
Despite what people say.
We are one big family
Living on this earth.
This I do believe
For what it's worth.

The Last Supper

They said, "Now he* belongs to the ages,"
As he took his final breath.
At least he was with family
(An ignoble death.)
It doesn't really matter
What you say or do.
The maggots come to eat you
As if you were a stew.

*Abraham Lincoln (1809-1865), the 16th president of the United States. He was assassinated at Ford's Theatre while watching the play, *Our American Cousin,* and died across the street at Peterson's House ("the house where Lincoln died") on April 14, 1865. He freed the slaves and made us all free.

My Defibrillator

If I could put into words
The meaning of true love,
I would have to say to you
They're none of the above.
Oh, how you make me feel inside.
You bring exhilaration.
But most of all I find in you
My defibrillation.

Polite Conversation (P.C.)

I can't say the 'bee' word.
It is "incorrect."
In fact, it is a communist plot
To ever disrespect
Another human being
Although I do not know
Another way to say it.
I like my bungalow.

Career Counseling and Placement

When I was ten I took a pen
And wrote my first short poem.
I don't know why I was so shy
I never even showed them.
Years went by (how do they fly)
I was the last to know it.
I thank God for my iPod
And that I am a poet.

A Singular Sensation

If I have a single friend,
I know it would be you.
And I know within my heart
You will always be true.
But you think my avoirdupois
Is very ordinary.
Don't you think in my own way
I'm very extraordinary?

This Model-T

Sometimes I have a jealous heart.
Sometimes it really shows
When I look upon my neighbor
And covet his new clothes.
But this sheepskin on my back
Is all I can afford
And explains (in part)
Why I drive a Ford.

Macabre

A Misspent Youth

I thought my life had ended.
What else could I do?
My salad days were over.
I knew it was true.
I did not best in every way
Although I do not know
If perchance it was enough
To wildly seedling sow.

A Near-Death Experience

Suddenly it hit me
Right between the eyes.
There was no mistaking.
There was no disguise.
The doctor whispered to me
I had nearly died
And had almost escaped
To the other side.

Suicide Note (Form: 1066)

Name:_____
Date:_____
Social Security Number:_____

Dear John: 3:16

Without or without warning
It knew it had to end.
But in spite of this
It will now depend
On a higher being
Who is my best friend.
Self-slaughter is not sanctioned.
But this I do defend.

The Food Chain

All that's left is kibbles
At the bottom of the bowl.
Tabby looks at me and snivels
As if on the dole.
I give to her more Cat Chow.
She looks as if to say,
"I love you, my dear mommy.
Now let's go and play."

The Cat Fight

First I do regret
I could not be there
For the pugilistic
Battle and the fanfare.
But I could see the tufts
Lying on the floor.
I can only hope
They do this no more.

"Verily, verily, I say unto you…"

I am the Devil's advocate.
You should not believe
Anything I say or do.
You will be deceived.
Honesty is very
Difficult to find.
The hardest thing in this world
Is to speak your mind.

Otology*

St. Vincent+ and St. Paul++
Came to lose their ears
In different situations
As it now appears.
Vincent was the butcher.
But J. Paul I revere
Because he had so much to lose
And so much to fear.

*The branch of medicine that deals with the anatomy, functions and diseases of the ear. (OED).
+Vincent van Gogh (1853-1892), maladjusted postimpressionist artist who killed himself with an unregistered handgun. He was shot to hell.
++J. Paul Getty III, heir to the of the fabulous Getty fortune. He was kidnapped in 1973 and was held for a $17 million ransom (losing his ear in the end game).

The Pine Forest

Endless are the days
That I pine for you.
Truancy is something
I can't get used to.
You told me you were leaving
And never coming back.
They say that burning bridges
Can cause a heart attack.

"Get Into the Groove"

Platitudes and homilies
I can do without.
They sweeten and they sour
But never do amount
To much of anything
That I can approve
Unless, of course, you find yourself
Getting in the groove.

The Advice Not Taken

If you can afford it,
Why settle for less?
Value is not something
You can second-guess.
Mother always told me
Always do your best
And never do anything
You cannot confess.

A Conundrum

"Quality versus quantity?"
The slogan is not new
To those of us alive today.
It is your point of view
That predicts the answer
That you do pursue.
"Quality versus quantity?"
What's a girl to do?

Fat Cats, Sr.*

I have to feed the kitties.
They are getting thin.
Malnutrition in the feline
Is a mortal sin.
I give to them their Crunchies
At exactly half past two.
Voracious is their nature.
I watched as they grew.

*cf. Fat Cats, Jr, (p. 50).

Philanthropy

We want to serve the people
But we don't know how.
We do all we can
That we can do now.
But good will will not help us
Help the helpless man.
We misunderstand him.
We're a flash in the pan.

A Tropical Depression

Melancholy lady,
I am so depressed
Really over nothing
That I can attest.
Moodiness is something
I cannot control.
Just be on the lookout
So as to console.

The Trust Fund

Trust is really something
That you have to earn.
No matter how you try
You can never learn
It inside a classroom
Or a lecture hall
But once you have found it
You will have a ball.

Rigor mortis

I was the exception.
Now I am the rule.
There is no accepting
What I'm going through.
Don't misunderstand me.
I have been a fool.
I merely tried to bend
The rigid Golden Rule.

A Frugal Repast?

Dinnertime is sacred
At the Martin house.
Pot roast and potatoes
A la Levi Strauss.
Don't look at me and wonder
What I ate tonight.
I will gladly tell you
It was not light.

Prisoner of Love

I try not to disappoint you.
But I think I have.
I personally think you treat me
Like your personal slave.
I could never understand
What I mean to you.
I do everything
That you want me to.

Part I

Part III

A Cat's Heart 47
The First Person Singular 47
"Separate but Equal" 47
Callousness 48
The Visionary 48
Damaged Goods 48
The Piano Man 49
Recognizance 50
Trust Issues 50
Fat Cats, Jr. 50
"The Do-Gooder" 51
Etude 1: Metaphor and Simile as Autobiography 52
Etude 2: The End of Slavery 52
Etude 3: Only on a First-Name Basis 52
Etude 4: An Isolated Incident 52
Etude 5: "2x Shy:" The Birth of Cynicism 52
Global Warming ☺ 53
"A Lucky Seven" 54
In God's Image? 54
"Indefatigable" 54
Shortchanged 55
Historiography as "Ancestuousness" 56
The Starter Wife 56
The Lonely Night 56
A Baker's Dozen 57
Static Cling: My Philosophy (1988) 58
Static Cling: My Philosophy (1998) 58
Static Cling: My Philosophy (2008) 58
"I Know" 59
Salvation 59
The Wisdom of the Ages 59
"A Draw" 60
Deaf Ears 60
Unfathomable 60
Obsequiousness 61
Stop the Bull! 61
Love: The Overture 61
The Rust Belt 62
Xenophobia 62
That's That 62

Part II

All Words 29
"The Greatest Show on Earth" 29
Audacity 29
Dexter the Dexterous 30
Free Speech 30
The Reluctant Reformer 30
"Pam's Best Friend" 31
Felicitations 32
Nocturnal Emission 32
Funny Money (☺$$$) 32
Queen Nefertiti 33
Limericks: The Hang Over 34
Limericks: Homophobia 34
Limericks: Ich-Theology 34
Limericks: "The Urge to Expand" 34
The Love Train 35
U.T.I. 36
A Sympathy Vote 36
Forewarned 36
Bunk Beds 37
A Fascist Ballad 38
Infidel 38
Am I Alive? 38
Turning Back Time 39
A Life Decision 40
The Gaming Commission 40
"The Impossible Dream" 40
Plate Tectonics 41
Recriminations 41
Died-in-the Wool 41
The Labyrinth of Life 42
A Better Life 42
"Dear" 42
A Profile in Courage 43
Corpulence 43
Polyglot 43

Table of Contents

Part I

Rigor mortis 11
A Frugal Repast? 11
Prisoner of Love 11
Philanthropy 12
A Tropical Depression 12
The Trust Fund 12
Fat Cats, Sr. 13
Get Into the Groove 14
The Advice Not Taken 14
A Conundrum 14
The Pine Forest 15
The Cat Fight 16
"Verily, verily, I say unto you…" 16
Otology 16
The Food Chain 17
Macabre: A Misspent Youth 18
Macabre: A Near-Death Experience 18
Macabre: Suicide Note (Form: 1066) 18
This Model-T 19
Polite Conversation (P.C.) 20
Career Counseling and Placement 20
A Singular Sensation 20
My Defibrillator 21
Twin Daughters of Different Litters 22
The Family of Man 22
The Last Supper 22
The Oedipus Complex 23
"All the News that's Fit to Print" 23
Homer 23
Anthropology 101: *Novis Homo* 24
Anthropology 101: The American Adam 24
Anthropology 101: The Greasy Spoon 24
Abraham, Abraham 25
Relapses 25
I'll be damned! 25

For Bob

A Baker's Dozen
Copyright 2008 by Pamela Gowan

All rights reserved under International and Pan-American copyright conventions. No part of this book may be reproduced, stored in a retrieval system or transmitted in any form, electronic, mechanical, or by any other means, without written permission of the author.

Illustrated by Kathleen Hardy.

International Standard Book Number: 978-0-615-26193-5

A Baker's Dozen

Poems by

Pamela Martin

www.ingramcontent.com/pod-product-compliance
Lightning Source LLC
Chambersburg PA
CBHW021238090426
42740CB00006B/591